Neural Masseur

Matt Langley

BookLeaf
Publishing
India | USA | UK

Presentation by *BookLeaf Publishing*

Web: www.bookleafpub.com

E-mail: info@bookleafpub.com

ISBN: 9789358311808

First edition 2023

ACKNOWLEDGEMENT

I must acknowledge Ailsa, who sent me the link that motivated this project. I am eternally grateful that she inspired me to try.

I must also acknowledge my tireless muse (and collaborator), Sheryl Weller, who has read so many of my ramblings, yet has encouraged me to keep on rambling.

PREFACE

There is no overarching theme to these poems, although many of them are about relationship to other people's minds, hearts, souls and spirits. I wrote from my heart and trusted that my emotions would translate well on the page.

I hope you find them moving in some way.

Confidants

When our spirits project into the unknown
And we willingly go for the ride
It may be that new truths about us are shown`
Leaving nothing more for us to hide

Baring our souls to someone we trust
Letting all of our secrets lay bare
Discretion between us becoming a must
As innermost feelings we share

Likely reality isn't quite so…
We still may be feeling selective
Our deepest sentiments soon we will show
Becoming more bold; less protective

Having someone who listens is gold
As the traumas we've kept to ourselves now
unfold

Dissolution

2

Two-thirds
Of a lifetime
Astounding, the number
Representing something vanished;
Let go...

Rose Garden

On a tiny plot of fertile soil,
A rose garden blooms bright
Only three bushes fit
On the strip of ground so tight

Their glistening hearty leaves
Their thick and thorny stems
Pale against the vibrant buds
That bloom from each of them

The first is full but wispy
Strong but fragile is its frame
Fewer thorns than the others bear
By all appearances, tame

She blooms in yellow, pink and orange
Rainbow sherbet comes to mind
Refreshing, sweet and delicate
Gorgeous blossoms, so sublime

The next rose towers above them all
Stems that bulge and swell
Enormous blooms, petals proud
Cast an exotic spell

The blossoms on this second one
Are lavender perfumed
The giant thorns on every stalk
Suggest you give them room

A third rose bush stands next to them
Each stem ridden with tiny thorns
This one still is growing tall
Having been the last one born

Its blossoms pulsate fragrance
From petals red like wine
Stealing attention from the others
With a radiance divine

They fill the space they're growing in
With ebullience and mirth
Drawing happy smiles from everyone
Who passes their patch of earth

The three rose sisters stand as one
Displaying all their glory
Their beauty not to be denied
A sisterhood…a story

Paradox

Self love?
What does that mean?
Abandon the ego,
Yet still show fondness for one's self?
Do tell…

Tele(pathy)gram!

An image sprouts and blossoms in the mind
Or maybe it's from the spirit
Harvested and sent aloft
Not everyone can hear it

Adrift on a course through the ether
Intended for someone's delight
It might take a day to get there
It may take one whole night

Arrival goes unheeded
Receiver does not even know
Once the thought has been delivered
Straight to her heart it flows

Warm wave of contentment
Creates a peaceful calm
Envelops a heart with gratitude
Though she has no idea where it's from

Is this feeling random
What has caused these sudden joys
She marvels at this momentary
Clarity among the noise

A sentiment shared from far away
Without pencil, pen or phone
A thought released, a loving wish
Has found its proper home

The Voice

Dormant microphone
Stands by stoically on call
Seats begin to fill

Check check one two three
Dulcet voice rends the stillness
Kickoff imminent

Ladies, gentlemen
Welcoming all who attend
Contest has begun

Deep resonant tone
Floods the autumn night time buzz
Booming from on high

Faceless narrator
Filling ears with play by play
Touchdown, Santa Rosa!

Fight song rumbles forth
Orange and black celebration
And…the kick is good!

Win, lose…either way

Rosa fans leave satisfied
From another game

Voice of an icon
Kept their spirits in the game
Now bids them Adieu

Goodnight, thank you all
For everlasting support
Of Panther Football
And remember fans
As you head out on the road
Please drive safely

'Til next Friday night
Once again placed to the side
Microphone dormant

Connections

To what force in the universe
Do I owe this exquisite pleasure
Random chance becoming real
A gift transforms to treasure

Curiosity turns to desire
Not tawdry craving for carnal delight
A longing, instead, to share one's soul
With one who makes days bright

To have good fortune such as this
Garnering a trusting bond
Constant communication
Develops a connection quite fond

And who'd have guessed some time ago
There ever would have been
Friendship echoes from long ago
Rekindled from way back when

Take the chance, reach out with love
Don't hesitate to inquire
Let someone know, who won't expect,
That your soul they do inspire!

Manifest love of the dearest kind
Warm and safe and free
Open your heart, your mind, your soul
As wide as they can be.

For in this state we change the world
Make it better than before
Invite another soul to walk with you
Through destiny's golden door.

If

If dying now meant I could be
Preserved here preternaturally
Not shuffled to some other plane
Body gone, but spirit remained
Perched right here upon this hill
Then I would exercise my will
Tell the universe to go ahead
Take my life, proclaim me dead
Here I'll stay, mild alpine heat
The breeze so cool, the cherries sweet
I'll watch this game forevermore
Urging the Wicked to tie the score
Beaming with joy and pride and love
Each time my Phil wields her mighty glove
Sun suspended at high noon
This contest ending no time soon
I'll root and shout, laugh and cry
As eternity saunters by

Beamish Boy

Open
Giving, loving
Placid blue eyes aglow
Reaching deeply into your soul
Tranquil

Sweet smile
Attracting all
To revel in its warmth
Absorb the purely innocent
Kindness

Still here
Much older man
Although at heart, still three
Yearns to spread that transforming light
Far…wide

Gaze deep
Your heart infused
Unconditional love
Cheers spirit exponentially
A gift

Allow

Great surge of joy
To occupy your soul
Smiling back at his boyish eyes
Know peace

Yet Again...

The maelstrom gathers silently,
Ions tiptoeing the perimeter surreptitiously
With painstaking nonchalance

"Nothing to see here, unwitting victim,"
They whisper as they lurk,
"No cause to be alarmed!" they lie.

One bloodshot eye
Standing sentinel for yet another anxious hour
Relaxes its cramping lid,
Inviting sleep quietly inside
To bring its rejuvenating magic to bear
Inside the cautious mind

Yet again…

The coast is clear.
The wraiths of chronic anxiety
Scurry quickly to assemble in
Their unrelenting phalanx

They bide their time
Swords and spears at rest,
But stand ready

Ever ready

The neural masseurs of Slumberland
Fully engaged in their business
Of soothing the swollen synapses
Throbbing with exhaustion and overuse
Are present to heal,
Bent to their delicate work
With absolute dedication.

Yet again…

They fail to sense the imminent

Out of blind faith, the doors
Entrusted to protect the sacred chamber
Are never locked securely
Soon they will be torn from their hinges
As the maelstrom commences its siege

The masseurs all flee in terror
And the tender guardians of soothing sleep
Are entirely chased away
Leaving behind all that they brought with them
To be collected in the aftermath

Thunderbolts of inadequacy
And crippling self-doubt

Resound and echo from the walls
Of inner consciousness
The swords of grief
The piercing arrows of regret
Swirling gales of pessimism
Eradicate any evidence
That restfulness was ever present

Yet again…

Both bloodshot eyes strain,
Their lids pressed together
In a futile effort to deny
The maelstrom its victory.
But…to no avail.

As the peaceful calm
Is torn asunder
The bloodshot eyes pop open and
A new day begins
Far, far too early…

Yet again…

July

Brilliant rays make shadows dance
Cool breeze rattles the heart-shaped leaves
Mesmerizing concrete light show
Captivates the aimless mind
Free, if for only one moment,
Of other cares and woes

Summer heat is resting
Banking its intensity for another day
Releasing just enough to give the day
A tolerable edge
Sweating icy drink stands by
Poised to refresh a growing thirst

Sprinklers spray their cooling fan
Mist hovering above the lawn
The droplets split the spectrum
Rainbows dance among the spray
Gleeful squeals fill the air
Children frolicking gleefully

Distant aroma of charcoal fire
Arrives to tint the lilting air
Promises of grilled delights
Punctuate the carefree afternoon

Enticing all who share the smell
To break bread with one another

Darkness will be held at bay
Daylight properly stretched and fit
To run the marathon of a summer day
Sun lazily drifting across the sky
Taking its sweet time to elongate
The pleasures of its presence

Still, the undulating shadows
Captivate the empty mind
Inexhaustible leaves continue their dance
Projecting on the ground
Nature's art installment
Soothing my weary soul

Old Forester 110

Three wishes…

The first, to feel more relaxed
Granted in an instant
Stress subsides and I can breathe
Calm prevails

Feeling happier is the second
Wish to be fulfilled
Instantly accomplished
In a second amber flash

To have more freedom
Is next in line
Fruition takes much longer
But it happens over time…

There's a genie in every bottle, but...
Be careful what you wish for!

Love Buds

I took her last line as though writ for me
My heart swelled as the buds began to stir
I aimed my mind inside myself to see
Found what I thought I knew was just a blur

Cruel cacophony of my inner self
Strains the ear and dulls the curious eye
The swelling buds obscured upon a shelf
I reach, but they might be a bit too high

And all at once there comes a peace, a calm
It speaks to me; it was there all along:
To love myself for who I really am
The bud humming the most delightful song

And when it bursts into its vibrant flower
My heart discovers its potential power.

How Much Longer

Patience
Stolid virtue
At what point does the wait
Dwindle to mere futility
Folly

Transmission

Two sets of cobalt blue eyes meet
One pair bubbles with innocence of youth
The other emanating ages of wisdom
Both channeling the cosmic network of souls

She heard his voice, she knows she did
But his words evaporated
Like so many drops of water
From a hot cast iron pan

Frozen in time, adrift
In her own vast and private sea,
She struggles to remember…
But it's gone as gone can be

He sees her standing all alone
In the middle of the space
Staring off at nothing
Lost in her tiny corner of the infinite universe
Clueless and afraid
With empathy he softly calls her name

The echo of his timbre
Reverberates amid the blackness
Calling her back to a presence in the room

Head swivels, and she sees him beckon
An involuntary smile
Curls her relieved and grateful face

Motioning for her to sit
He quietly takes a knee
Dropping to her level
So each other's eyes they'll see
Some tacit protocol tells her
Exactly how to receive
Her eyelids snap wide open
Prepared to not once blink
He closes his own eyelids
And draws a clearing breath
Opens them after after a moment of calm
And fixes her gaze with his

Their placid smiles indicate
What's going on beneath
The physical world's rigid facade
As they meet each other's minds
He doesn't try to occupy
Her fragile youthful soul
Instead he simply visualizes
What he wants her now to do
Image transmitted effortlessly
Her paths are open wide
There is no doubt it will reach its mark
A wider smile stretches her face

As all becomes so clear
As she receives it fully
The image vanishes from his mind
His eyes close tightly shut
As he steps back into consciousness

He watches as she gets to work
A carbon copy of
Exactly what he sent
In painstaking detail
A telepathic fax

This scene plays out over many more days
Once he becomes aware
That she sees a world, just like him,
Others don't know is there

Frozen

Trapped
Or so it feels
Sitting anemic and silent
Absorbing words of passion
Words of devotion
Words of doubt
Words of confusion
Words spoken by a lover
Causing other words to sprout inside my
paralyzed mind
That won't find their way out
Into the open air
Catching in my throat and dissolving into
A perception that I have nothing in response
That I don't care
That she is right
That I'm not worthy of her love
That I am suppressing secrets
That stand in the way of a future
Stultifying fear masquerades
As stoic silence
A guise of heartlessness that
Couldn't be less true

BEI

Stretching far and wide below
Nighttime San Franciscan sprawl
Glimmers through the panes of glass
But will they heed the call

Romance beckons in the air
Curtains open wide
The mesmerizing urban glow
Affecting love's mood inside

This luxurious space eleven floors
Above the bustling streets
Intimate setting, undeniably poised
Urging their hearts to meet

Glorious, irresistible
Succumbing to the night
Entangling their disparate lives
Amid the ambient city light

Afterglow augments the scene
Adding depth to the urban glare
Radiance kindled of pure passion
Again, it soon will flare

Declaration

It took
Me by surprise,
Declaring love had died,
Gave me no chance to find my way
Back home

Discretion

How long must this be stifled underground
When can we bring it out into the light
To secrecy we currently feel bound
Slow dance obscured by shadows of the night

Far too complicated are the reasons
Which keep this from becoming public news
Likely we will live through two more seasons
Before exhilaration draws its due

Til then, the thrill of secrecy will bring
A piquant spice to this grand rendezvous
Two hearts, apart from others, made to sing
Alone, and yet together, ringing true

Time is soon to come for the big reveal
Until that time, we help each other heal.

Indelible

Stitched to his heart like a badge of honor
That will travel with him wherever he goes
From this day forth
The memory of an image
Tattooed on his psyche
Never to be removed

Amid an opaque fog of confusion
The palpable miasma of awkward exchanges
She escapes to the solace of a safe space
Which he dares not pursue
Lest irreversible damage befall a connection
So precious and uplifting
He should not be here, he knows that now
A truth that dawns too late
Illuminating the icy air,
Spot lit by its undeniable veracity

The game ended, the intruder seeks her out
Approaching with an air of caution
Desperately hoping not to frighten away
She who is already poised to bolt
There is so much that longs to be said

Yet words stick in their throats like cotton balls
And stammered efforts to make sense
Freeze and fall on frigid asphalt
If only he could make her understand
Help her see that he has not arrived
To prey upon her sacred privacy
But simply to feel a physical presence,
A physical and present manifestation
Of the joy they've shared across 500 miles

He finds a phrase
A term he employs to display
He really, truly sees her for who she is
Appreciates the reason why she feels the need
To disappear and disengage
It travels from his lips, miraculously
Three short words
Whose meaning she has taught him all about
Three words that help define herself
Land softly in her ear
Somehow slipping past the jumbled words
She speaks in her agitated state
They land, and there is silence
For just a moment
She looks at him, and their eyes meet
The smile that overtakes her mouth
Makes her lovely face convey
The contents of her beauty-ridden heart

Its purity and kindness
A childlike smile from her most innocent days
Makes every awkward moment worth it
In that momentary stillness
She is seen
A smile never to be forgotten
Indelible

Face Forward

Focus fully aimed on the rearview mirror
Left no option but to crash
Repeatedly wrapping a life around a tree
Or plunging from yet another cliff
Or hitting a fellow distracted driver head on
Obliterating their life too, in time,
Resulting in pieces scattered far and wide
Picking them up over and over again
Rebuilding something shattered, ever weaker
than before
Only to continue driving forward
With attention rooted deeply in the past
An accident waiting, no…DETERMINED to
happen
I've snapped that rearview mirror off
Torn off the side mirrors as well
Discipline required to keep facing forward
Becomes easier with each revolution
Of the hands around the clock
The view is spectacular ahead of you
Wide open, diverse, possibilities abound
So much more to experience in front of you
Than that narrow view you were addicted to
In the rearview mirror